August 1st, 2___

My Journey to the New World

GUDRUN HONIG

To an old friend;
thanks you for
recognizing us!
Gudrun Honig.

ACKNOWLEDGMENTS

Some of my friends insisted that I should write down events from my life because they sounded so interesting. I really had no idea how to go about it. However, as I paged through the University of British Columbia Continuing Studies catalogue, the program, "Journal Writing & Voice of One's Own" seemed worth a try. Thank you, dear Professor Marlene Schiwy for your guidance.

I would like to express my appreciation to the ladies at the front desk at the Hollyburn Country Club in West Vancouver, Eloise, Esthi, Donna, Samantha and Elanez (Ellie), for their encouragement and interest in my book as it came into being; the staff at Lens and Shutter in Park Royal, West Vancouver, who restored and enlarged the tiny Leica photos for the illustrations; last but not least my editor, David Shrimpton and my three adult sons, Peter, Paul and Mark who helped me with the new technology. Paul was able to retrieve the lost pages of my manuscript back on the screen to my great relief. Without the help of my family I could not have done it.

PART I

For the start of the story of my Journal, I have chosen not a chronological approach, but the final months of World War II: the invasion by the Americans into our quiet German farming community of Buechold near Hammelburg (see map). Hammelburg was and still is a military base. It was on Easter Sunday, 1944. I had been invited by my *Tante* (aunt) Marie, for the special Easter lunch: home-raised baby goat and all the trimmings. Suddenly, there was a big noise outside the front door. Two fully armed unknown soldiers rushed by our kitchen. They went up the stairs. After a short time they entered the kitchen.

"Wann haben die deutschen Soldaten das Dorf verlassen?" (When did your soldiers leave this village?"), an American officer demanded to know, looking at me. I was very frightened. I expected to be raped. We had been warned that this would be the fate of young women, just as the Russian soldiers had raped them on their way to the west. I was very slow with my answer. I could see by the expression on their faces that the Americans did not believe me. As they were leaving, the superior officer smiled at me and handed me a bar of chocolate. I took the chocolate and smiled back at him.

It was my turn to rush upstairs and to look out of the window. I saw a long line of our soldiers walking slowly along the road to Hammelburg accompanied by American vehicles. They had become prisoners of war. I felt very sad. It was years later that I put two and two together and saw the connection of the above events. General Patton, the commander of the Third Army on his advance into Germany, organised a detour to the prisoner-of-war camp at Hammelburg. He wanted to free some American prisoners including his son-in-law. There are slightly different versions of this incident. I like to think that it was the General himself who dropped in on us on his way there and gave me the chocolate bar.

Shortly before the invasion of the Americans into my aunt's house in Buechold, I was walking in the open fields on my own. Suddenly, a lone flying single-engine plane buzzed about and targeted me. As its bullets hit the ground, I had the presence of mind to run for cover into the near-by bushes. I prayed to God. Not only did I survive this attack on my life, but everything else during the war. To think about it: I am in fact, a survivor of the war.

Later, both the German and American forces abandoned the military depot at Hammelburg and the locals looted the base. Some farmers filled their vehicles with military clothing, blankets, etc. I cycled to the depot, filled my pockets with

some odds and ends, took a new set of skis, loaded them on my bike and walked most of the way back. I still use the sewing thread that I took in 1944 because it is stronger than the thread I get now.

I have to turn to local history now. The expansion of the military base Hammelburg in 1937 changed the lives of the inhabitants of the two adjacent villages. Markers set the date of the founding of the village of Hundsfelt and Bonnland at 700. My mother's family name was Winter, a name that goes back a long way in the register the village.

The money paid to the farmers as compensation for their lost land was totally inadequate. They lost contact with their relatives and neighbours. In a class-action suit after the war, further compensation was awarded to the evicted farmers and families. My mother received one thousand Deutsch Mark. To my Dad's amazement she went to the International Fur Exhibition in Frankfurt and bought herself an elegant fur coat. In retrospect I applaud her for her courage to have her own mind. Eventually, my Dad resigned himself and rightly said: "Therese, you can do what you want with your money." She really looked beautiful, I think. My mother was a natural beauty in her younger days. She had wavy red hair and a white skin. When she entered a crowded room like in the Appelwine (cider) pubs in Sachsenhausen, there would be a short silence in the noisy hum as all eyes turned to her. Her two older sisters were well aware how her beauty attracted men. When the German soldiers were doing their military training at the base, they would march through Buechold. The three young girls would watch them march by. Marie and Christine could see the eyes of the soldiers staring at their younger sister. This made them very jealous! No, no, dear reader, do not jump to conclusions; they did not cut her my mother's hair off. The two 'ugly' sisters dyed Mama's red hair black with ink! Sounds like one of Brothers Grimm fairy-tale stories and I have not even talked about these characters in my life. Have no fear, dear Reader, we will meet them later.

Theresa, Marie and Christine – my mother and aunts

I have to add another personal note here regarding my dear Mama. Some of the evicted older farmers decided not to go back to farming and instead moved to the cities. I remember one of the old-timers was a frequent visitor when I was small. He continued telling my Mama that she was of the nobility, but she just laughed. Yet, this rumour is certainly believable. It is known that during the Thirty Year War (1618-1648) and other uprisings, the nobility went into hiding among the peasants. I like to believe the old-timer's story and to think that my ancestors might have owned one of these old now-ruined castles, which are still to be seen in the area.

Burg Saaleck in Hammelburg

My imagination tells me about the young maiden standing on top of the tower a-sighing:

"How lucky you are, falcon! You can fly wherever you like;
In the forest you can choose any tree that pleases you.
That is what I have done too:
I chose a man for myself, my eyes made the choice.
Now beautiful women are jealous of it.
Oh, why don't they leave me my lover?
After all, I have never wanted any lover of theirs!"
She may promise to be faithful and say:
"You are mine, I am yours, you may be sure of that.
You are locked in my heart; the key is lost.
You will have to stay inside it for ever".

Anonymous (The Penguin Book of German Verse, 1957.)

I have to give now even more historical details of my mother's background in order to clarify the coming events. When my maternal grandfather retired from farming in 1928, his medium-sized farm in Hundsfeld was divided among his three daughters. As my Tante Marie was the oldest, she received most of the farm. Tante Christine had married a farmer, she was very happy to inherit more land to add to their small acreage. Therese, my Mama, had moved to town when her oldest sister married. It was agreed between her and my aunt Marie that I could stay with her on the farm in the summer. Marie would have the crop of my Mama's fields in return.

Unton and Magdalena Winter – my grandparents

I must also mention the other village that was confiscated by the German Reich: Bonnland. According to the chronicle of Bonnland, a large country house stood there. The couple who lived there were great admirers of Friedrich von Schiller, a famous poet (1759 – 1805). In fact, the history seems to say that

9

the wife of the owner was a relative of the poet, who liked to visit the place. There were many books, artifacts and a bust of the poet on display. (Publisher and Supplier August Keller, Wasserdorf 57, 8711 Seinsheim).

Here is a famous poem by the poet Friedrich von Schiller, a contemporary of Johannes Wolfgang von Goethe (1749 – 1812).

The Lay of the Bell

The mould of baked clay stands firmly bedded in the ground.
The bell must be cast today.
The sweat will have to run from your hot faces.
If the job is to be a credit to the master, but the blessing on it
Comes from on high
Now with the power of the rope heave the bell up out of the pit,
To let it rise into the realm of sound into the air of heaven!
Pull, pull, heave. It moves, it hangs free.
May its first peal bring joy to this town, may it mean peace!"

(Penguin Book of German Verse introduced, edited and translated by Leonard Forster 1959. First and last verse only).

Johann Wolfgang von Goethe was born in Frankfurt am Main, although he lived most of his life in Weimar, helping the monarch with the affairs of the court. Since Frankfurt is also my home town, I will write a bit more about our famous citizen and Frankfurt. He made a journey to Italy, which introduced him to antiquity. I remember seeing a huge painting of him in the foyer of the Goethe Museum in Frankfurt. Goethe put German poetry on the map of Europe.

Mignon

Do you know the country where the lemon-trees flower,
and the golden oranges grow in the dark foliage,

where a gentle wind blows from the blue sky,
where the myrtle stands quiet and the bay-tree towers up?
Do you know it?
That is where, that is where, that is where,
I would like to go with you, O my beloved!

(The Penguin Book of German Verse. Introduction, edited and translated by Leonard Foster. First verse only).

The Goethe Museum is located on the banks of the river Main where the cathedral and most of our museums are. The historic sites and cathedrals of all the major European cities display a similar layout: London, Paris, Amsterdam, and Budapest, but not Moscow. For that reason, I try to find hotel accommodation close by. It saves a traveller a good deal of time and frustration by not having to use public transport or taxis. I am thinking now of an international hotel chain which has provided me with a nice continental breakfast. The foreign manager topped it up with delicious home-made light cake. The other bonus was that at breakfast time I saw the hotel guests. It seemed to me that each year another wave of new immigrants from a different country had arrived. They might be newcomers, but they were smart to have chosen this international budget hotel.

I often walked along the river. The Main is slow flowing, because of the dam further down, and is used by barges to transport goods. I now recall a neighbour from Westhausen who told me her daughter and ten children lived on a barge. In the summer sightseeing ships go from the Cathedral to the Rhein or Mosel with frequent stops along the route. I suppose one can still get off the ship and taste the local wine in one of the many restaurants.

Papa explained to me that Frankfurt was founded by the Frank tribes. They were trying to cross the wide river and luckily found a ford which allowed them to guide their horses safely through the waters. Papa was such a proud Frankfurter and always had many stories to tell. Occasionally, he would take a photo with his beloved Leica camera such as the view of the roof tops and the Roemer. These shots were taken before the buildings were destroyed by enemy bombs in 1944.

On a walkabout through the old town I passed the Judengasse (Jewish Lane). Browsing through old books last week in a store, I happened to come across a book with the title "Die Rothschilds". The old book describes in detail the rise of the Rothschild family in the town of Frankfurt and later in the world. The biography includes some photos which are also shown. (Egon Caesar Conte Corti: Die Rothschilds. Des Hauses Aufstieg Bluetezeit und Erbe). Heyne Biographies. Wilhelm Heyne Verlag Muenchen: Frankfurter Judengasse in the Moonlight, the Frankfurt Stock Exchange 19th Century).

Our favourite place was the Palmengarden. Papa had a free pass for the botanical garden and the zoo, because he worked for the city of Frankfurt. We made good use of it. The afternoon concerts given by the city orchestra were very popular. His love for music had not gone away, even though he had not played an instrument since my mother had her nervous breakdown.

My family: Regine, Gudrun, Theresa and Theodore in the Palmengarten

I loved to go to the Palmengarden. I was allowed to row on the pond by myself. To think about it, even at an early age I wanted to do my own thing. At the botanical garden I liked the relaxed atmosphere of people strolling about or sitting down on the wide terraces and having coffee and cake. Occasionally, we also sat down, so Papa generously ordered *Kaffee verkehrt* (more milk than coffee) for me. I felt very grown up.

Rowing in the Palmengarten in Frankfurt

Around Christmas, the Roemerplatz turned into an open air market crowded with shoppers on the lookout for home-made goodies. Hot drinks were in great demand: hot cider was of course a favourite. The many special Christmas lights illuminated the darkness and were for sale. The big bells of the dome counted out the hours of the day. Christmas markets are now all about. However, the Christmas market in Frankfurt is the most attractive one because of the location: the big square outside the cathedral and close the river and its bridges.

The Roemer in Frankfurt

Before we get lost, like Red Riding Hood did in the forest, I will turn to the family history of my father. Theodor Honig, comes from an entirely different background. He was born in Sandhausen near Heidelberg on April 22, 1906. On February 2, 1893 his father, Matthias Honig (born June 12, 1869) married Anna Maria Kopp (born December 19, 1870). They had eight children. I remember only three of Papa's siblings. Papa was not well disposed towards his father. He used to say that he was away a lot and left his mother to deal with all the children in a big flat in an old apartment block In Sachsenhausen, an older suburb of Frankfurt known for his excellent *Appelwein* (cider) and *Handkaes mit Music* (special marinated cheese with finely cut onions).

I remember family rumours that Matthias Honig, my grandfather on my father's side, had been a City Counsellor, so I inquired at the Institute for Stadtgeschichte. They confirmed that he was indeed a Counsellor from 1919 to 1924. The second rumour was that, before Papa was called into the Army, he had to appear twice before a special committee to prove his Arian heritage. Indeed, Papa looks very Jewish in an enlargement of an old passport photo taken when he was probably twenty-one years old.

Theodore

On closer reading of the history of Sandhausen, I came across a section which listed the religious denominations (Heimatbuch der Gemeinde Sandhausen 1986). There was a small Jewish community living in Sandhausen for over two hundred years. Until 1845 the community increased slowly, but then the population stopped growing. About that time, the Jewish people converted an old church into a Synagogue. My reasons for digging into the Jewish presence in Papa's birthplace are twofold: his Jewish looks on his passport photograph. Secondly, the family rumour of his investigation by a tribunal to check his background. I have come to the conclusion that there is a great possibility that he had Jewish roots. His father, Matthias Honig may have crossed over and married an Arian local village girl. There is also the possibility that he was classified as a privileged Jew, as his father had held a prominent position. Unfortunately, up to now, I can only guess but I will dig further (McLean's Magazine, November 19, 2010, Books: Berlin, and its Last Jews. Roger Moorhouse - Berlin at War).

The old box with photo of albums I had found in our basement puzzled me no end. I had forgotten that they were sent to me after my father died in 1983. I will enlarge these Leica photos and use them to illustrate my Journal. The next photo you see, dear Reader, is taken outside our small flat in Westhausen, a social housing estate outside Frankfurt. It shows me at age eight, my grandmother, mother, sister and cousin. Immediately I ask myself why I look so unhappy. What is bothering me? The events of my childhood came back slowly, but with my Dad's photographs they become a flood of memories. I intend to deal with my memories by writing about them in my journal. Maybe I shall find the answers to my questions "Who am I?", and "Where do I come from?"

Eight years old

I have come to the conclusion that my early life sounds like a fairy-tale by the Brothers Grimm, the German writers of these 18th century folk fairy-tales, which have become well-known to Western society through the films by Walt Disney. In modern versions of the stories all the tales started with the opening lines: "Once upon a time there was…" and ended with the words: "…and they lived happily ever after".

It is 200 years since that the first edition of the Fairy Tales was published. Ben Tarring a reporter with the Globe and Mail, a Canadian newspaper, went on the fairy-tale route of the Grimm Brothers' homeland (October 23, 2012). The city of Hanau near Frankfurt is the birth-place of the Brothers. The reporter emphasizes that it was the natural setting, the huge forests, which he considered the star of the tales, and observed that one had to leave a trail of white pebbles, like Haensel ("Hansel") did, to find your way out of them. What the journalist did not mention is the fact that one of the Brothers prepared the first German dictionary, but only reached the letter "F" of the alphabet: he died before he could finish the dictionary. However, others completed it.

Accompanying me on my journey to the New World, dear Reader, you may find that the characters which occurred in Red Riding Hood, Hansel and Gretel, Cinderella, and the main characters in the other fairy tales, one can encountered the real world as well. I met viscous wolves, bad and good fairies, but not an evil stepmother. In spite of it all, I was destined to meet my prince and "to live happily ever after".

My Tante Marie's promise to take me in the summer and look after me finally happened. I had looked forward to staying on the farm. Early in the morning I stepped out into the farmyard, because I enjoyed watching the chicken picking up the corn that had been thrown out for them. I suddenly cried out in horror, when I saw a headless cock racing around the farm yard. Apparently, the sharp axe had missed his neck, but eventually he was caught and ended up in kitchen pot. I could not eat the broth.

On my visit the following year, I heard noises downstairs in the barn. Stepping inside, I saw a frightening sight. Four men were bent over the rear end of a cow. Each had grabbed a leg of the calf sticking out and, with all their might, they tried to pull out the baby. The head should have come out first, but the calf had turned around inside the mother cow. The men cursed aloud, because they had been pulling for a long time. One of them looked up and saw me standing at the door. "Go into the house!" he commanded loudly. I could not go to sleep, as I could hear the men talking loudly inside the house. I was afraid of the unknown, but I found sleep, as I prayed to God. Because of the war, I did not go to the farm in the next year.

I have no photos of my infant brother, Gerhard. However, I remember him well, as he cried a lot when he got older. After his birth I got a baby doll as a present and so did Regine, my younger sister, who was four years younger than me. My doll was bigger than hers. While my mother was ironing one evening, Regine and I were watching her and hugging our dolls. Regine was constantly fussing, because she wanted my baby. Mama finally snapped at me: "Gudrun, why don't you give her your doll to hold for a while?" I very reluctantly handed her the doll, which she promptly dropped on the floor. Mama handed it back to me looking worried. The porcelain head had dropped off and I held in my arms the headless body of my only doll. Holding the headless baby in my arms, I shed many tears and hated my sister. The doll was later repaired.

I lost my baby brother when he was only nine months old. I remember standing around a deep hole in the ground when my brother in his wooden bed was lowered into the hole. I started to scream and run towards his grave. Dad came after me and picked me up. I noticed immediately that he was also crying.

Mama did not move or cry. Finally Papa took her by the hand and said: "It is time to go home, Therese".

It was shortly afterwards that Papa stopped practising his music. He even quit the symphony orchestra where he had played the bass in the string section. The instrument ended up on top of the linen cupboard and was forgotten. Great was my joy when I discovered the old bass standing in the living room of my niece, Lilo, in Frankfurt. She proudly pointed it out and said: "Opa's bass: I very much treasure this only antique piece I have. Tante Gudrun, do you remember Opa playing the bass?" How could I forget my dad embracing his beloved instrument and forever tuning it! "Yes, I do, it was too bad he had to give it up. After my little brother died, my mother had a nervous breakdown and did not want him to make music".

It was a full time job for the women at the time to run a home. To my mind they were always doing housework, like  Cinderella in the fairy tale of the same name. They had no modern appliances or hot water, which is the norm nowadays. We never had a daily bath. Once or twice during the week, water was heated by burning coal under a big cooper kettle and transferring it to the bathtub, where we had our backs scrubbed and hair washed. On other days, we took turns in our tiny upstairs bathroom with a hand basin to wash in cold water. Especially in the winter it got so cold in our flat that the inside of the windows were iced over.

Only after Papa bought up wood from the basement and coal to light the fire in our small oven, which heated the two-and-a-half room apartment, did we get up and get ready for the day. Here was no electric heat at all in any of these flats. In retrospect Mama and all the other women at the time were heroines, especially during the war. They did not hear from their husbands, who were fighting the enemy, for weeks or even months. I can see clearly before my eyes my dear Mama swinging her wedding ring over a photograph of Dad. When it moved, he was still alive. She would then relax with a sigh of relief and bravely carry on. Shopping was also difficult. There was a very small grocery shop just across the street from us, but Mama would not shop there, because of the poor selection of food and the fact that there always seemed to be gossipy women standing around in there.

On a walkway between the blocks of flats, I loved to play hopscotch. I jumped across the squares I chalked on the pavement with delight. Mama could watch me from her kitchen window. Next to us on the ground floor, lived a local soccer hero. He was socially much in demand and his young wife was alone a lot. She would watch me from her window from time to time with a smile on her face. On the day of the tragedy, she waved to me and drew her curtain. After a while, passers-by sniffed the air, but hurried on. Eventually, one man stopped and called out: "Gas" and rang all the door bells. Many doors opened, but not the soccer player's door. Eventually, the police came and carried my friend out on a stretcher. She did not survive and I missed her watching and smiling at me. The new tenants objected to my chalk drawings and I had to stop playing my game. With my older friends in my apartment block and the next one, we retaliated. As a group, we went Schellenklopfen (ringing the doorbells and running away).

Dear Reader, my next photo in the album, which is on the title page of the book, shows me with a smile. I had joined the Hitler youth. At the meetings we were sitting around the campfire, playing games and singing. When we were marching we sung loud and clear. Unsere Fahnen flattern voran (Our flags are waving in the wind, ahead of us) was my favorite

marching song. One Sunday we were given small white flags, bussed into town and joined other Hitler Youth lined along a wide tree-lined street. On command of our leader we waived our flags and shouted on top of our voices: "Heil Hitler" (Hail Hitler). A man in the brown uniform was standing up in the open car and saluted in reply. He was the leader of the pack of wolves, but we did not recognize him as such in his sheep's clothing. The ordinary people were all misled by his false promises. At that moment in time he gave our nation hope for a better future, like jobs and, above all, enough to eat. Of course the German youth was excited by this staged parade. We often talked about the rally and the Fuehrer, but did not know that he was the leader of the wolf pack.

It was during that time that I attended ballet classes in town. I was thrilled to be chosen to take part in the Christmas performance at the opera house as a mushroom in an enchanted forest in a fairy-tale by the Brothers Grimm called Haensel and

Gretel. The rehearsals unfortunately conflicted with my Saturday Hitler Jugend (Hitler Youth) meetings. After I had missed two meetings, the Youth leader called at our house demanding to know the reason for my absence. When Papa had finished explaining my absence, she requested to have it confirmed in writing by the opera house. I could see by Dad's face that he was very annoyed. By the year 1936 attendance at the Hitler Youth meetings were compulsory. I recently read that Hitler supported the fairy tales of the Brothers Grimm because they reflected nationalistic ideas: obedience, discipline, authoritarianism, militarism, glorification of violence (The New Yorker July 23, 2012).

We are lost and, like Haensel and Gretel, we have to go back to our starting point, namely our apartment in Westhausen. On the other side, of the walkway, were strips of lawn with upright posts on each end. These posts were used to fasten on the ropes to dry the wet laundry or to hang up carpets on specific days of the week. Carpets were cleaned with carpet beaters. On cleaning days the carpets produced a lot of noise and dust. We kept away on those days. The laundry was quite often laid out on the lawn for bleaching by the sun. It was my task then to water the laundry with a watering can. The nearest water source was in the basement, so I had to climb up and down the steep stairs to get the water. This bleaching process was not as bad as bringing the wet heavy laundry upstairs. The worst chore, however, was washing the laundry. No, no, there were no washing machines, vacuum cleaners or dishwashers; everything was done by hand. The very large copper kettle was heated with coals and the dirty washing was boiled and occasionally stirred. After a cooling-down period, the laundry was transferred into our bathtub and rinsed, transferred into buckets and carried upstairs. In nice weather it was all hung up outside or even spread out on the lawn. In bad weather the laundry was hung up in the drying room, which was surprisingly roomy.

In memory of the brave women of the last century, I turn to the Thirty Years War of 1618-1648. The main character is Mother Courage. It is also the title of this play by modern poet Brerthold Brecht (1898-1956). My university professor saw the mother as a war profiteer in the play, because of her bartering between the troops. I heard myself immediately loudly objecting. "To my understanding of the play", I heard myself say "Mother Courage is the prototype of all mothers during any war." I continued to argue that during World War II many mothers were desperate for food. They even went so far as to sell their bodies to obtain necessities. The learned professor did not object, but I continued my argument on the subject of the role of women in society, and said: "Where are the memorials on this campus to the countless heroines? All I can see are statues and inscriptions to heroes." In fact I had also missed monuments to the heroines of the war in Downing Street, in London, England. Dear Reader, I am glad to say that both on the campus at the University of British Columbia and in London one can now find monuments with inscriptions honouring the women of each World War for their services to their homeland.

I am proud to say, that it was at this point in my life I had discovered "a voice of my own." I was amazed, when another mature student complimented me and said: "Gudrun, you have done a great service to the feminist cause". The joke was that I counted myself among the traditional women at the time and the feminist movement was not an idea I was happy with.

What I must tell you now, is the beginning of terror in my former homeland. The leader of the pack of wolves, Adolf Hitler, decided to do away with Jews. On November 9, 1938, the terrible tragedy of Kristalnacht (night of broken glass) was enacted. Jewish homes and shops were ransacked; the occupants were beaten and arrested. Synagogues were burnt all over Germany by the wolf pack: the Storm Troopers also called the SS. We had in Frankfurt a large number of Jewish people; many of them living in the attractive west-end around the university. The wolves sniffed them out and rounded them up. Ethnic cleansing had started. Many of the Jewish people had left Germany in a hurry, but others were too slow or did not want to leave the country in which they had made their home. Concentration camps were their final destination.

A local railway track went by our allotment garden. When Mama worked in the garden, she allowed me to walk to the train track. Watching the closed cattle cars go by, now very slowly, gave me a sad feeling. Why were they suddenly so slowly? I felt that many eyes were watching me from the train and I was frightened. I quickly ran back to our garden and never went train-watching again.

When the mass deportation of Jews began in 1942, four students decided it was time to do something. According to the Vancouver "Prolifer" Newsletter of February, 2011, the students printed and distributed anti-fascist leaflets. They were arrested and condemned to death by the People's Court. The name of the street I lived on in Westhausen was changed after the war from New Guinea Way to Geschwister Scholl Strasse (Brother and Sister Scholl Street) in honour of the brother and sister team who tried to oppose the dictatorship of the Fuehrer. Besides Jews, Hitler also sent homosexuals, gypsies and handicapped people to their deaths.

I was wrong in my belief that the first bombs fell on Frankfurt in 1942. A hand-out by the City of Frankfurt am Main Institute of the City's History, states that the first air raid alarm went off as early as June 4, 1940. The first bombers came only at night. We immediately ran to our small local air-raid shelter, which for us was a converted basement in our block of flats; each of the twenty blocks of flats had only one air raid shelter. The targets for the bombers were the railway station and factories, none of which were in our neighborhood, but bombs also fell on houses away from those targets. As soon as the air-raid alarms sounded, I had stomach pains, no doubt caused by my fear. Later the enemy started to send planes during the day as well. More bombs now hit their targets. During an air-raid one of my older girl-friends went into town for a dental appointment, but did not return. I often went to her parent's house and looked over the garden fence, but I never saw her again. I missed her: she had been a good sport.

During the war our lights were dimmed at night and the window curtains drawn in an attempt to achieve Verdunklung (darkness). The City of Frankfurt built 38 large air-raid shelters. I remember that one of these bunkers received a direct hit from a bomb and everyone inside was killed. The worst raid was on March 18, 1944 towards the end of the war. According to the hand-out by the Institute for History of Frankfurt, the Royal British Air Force employed over a thousand bombers and attacked the inner city in six consecutive waves dropping thousands of bombs.

Considering the fact that in the centre of Frankfurt there were only housing, historical building, monuments, churches and museums, the question comes to my mind was not the bombing of women and children an act against humanity? I dare to say that Winston Churchill, the British Prime Minister at the time, was also a big bad wolf. No, no, he was not. He was a bloody 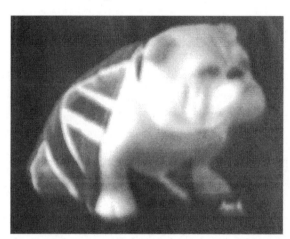 English bulldog. I did not think an English bulldog would exist in any English fairy tales like Alice in Wonderland, or any other tale. Churchill made a speech in which he threatened to wipe the German nation off the face of the earth. I will have to look again to find when and where he made this speech. A Canadian veteran argued with me recently that no statesman would ever make such a hateful speech! Maybe it is for this reason that his political party was not returned to power after the war.

The German authorities decided to remove school-children from the endangered cities to the safer countryside in 1942, when the air raids increased. Five schoolmates of mine volunteered to go with me to a school camp in Bavaria. There were 400 girls, two older female teachers and four youth leaders. We slept six in a room and there was not much supervision. One of my roommates discovered the storage room, where all the apples were kept. Hunger was our excuse for breaking into the room and taking away as many apples as we could carry. Luckily, we were not caught. Who knows what might have happened to us if we had been caught.

However, I did have a guilty conscience for quite a while. The food at the camp was actually not bad at all, however, it was not enough, nor was it like Mama's cooking. The missing ingredient in camp food was mother's love.

When Papa had to go into the army one year after the war started, Mama planned to make him his favourite cheese cake. She saved her food coupons to buy the ingredients. Yet in her haste and secrecy she mistook the pot of salt for a pot of sugar. The house was filled with her lamentations and Dad had a hard time pacifying her. I had watched her sitting on our window shelf, as I always did, kneading the dough and spreading the cheese mixed with the eggs on top - my mouth watered in anticipation, and after all her effort, there was no cheese cake, as the salt had ruined everything!

Cheese cake seems to be on top of the list of all cake lovers. My Tante Marie also made tasty cheese cake, called "platz" in their dialect. This cake was not really a cake because the dough was bread dough. Here goes the story. In Buechold the villagers shared a big wood-fired bread oven, as everyone baked their own bread. So when it was my Tante Marie's turn to make her bread in the community oven, she would spread cheese mixed with eggs on the stretched sheet of yeast dough, and it went into the hot oven. The "platz" was eaten warm; this invention by the clever housewives of Buechold tasted almost as good, as the cakes from finest pastry shops.

While talking about the clever housewives of Buechold, I must also tell you, dear Reader, about my cousin Paula. My cousin suffered from epilepsy. One day when she was at home cooking, she had a seizure and fell on the hot plate of the wood-fired stove. Her right forearm was badly burnt. On account of this accident, it was decided to have always somebody present when she was cooking or baking. She, too, was an excellent baker and her Christmas cookies were exceptional. She would bake them about four weeks in advance of the holidays and store them in some special tin boxes. This time Ignaz, her younger brother, was home to watch over her. He also watched where she put the cookie jars. When Christmas came, she went to her hiding place to get them. The jars were there but no cookies inside. The thief deserved the thrashing she gave him, but it hurt me too because I was watching.

Until 1942 the Blitzkrieg had served its purpose on the Eastern Front: our troops had advanced fast; our tanks had travelled as far as Stalingrad. However, with the arrival of winter, they came to a halt. Stalin had set a trap for the troops and they fell

into it. The heavy snow made it impossible for supplies to get through. Above all, many soldiers suffered from frostbite or worse. A high percentage of Dad's blood had been frozen and he was sent to a military hospital back in Germany, where all his blood was to be renewed over a period of time. He had even been put on the danger list. His two sisters went to visit him in the military hospital. In the home-bound train, they told a senior medical doctor about their brother and he promised them he would look into it. Indeed, Dad got better and Mama also visited him, as she was able to put my sister and me into a camp during her absence. I did not like it there and blame it on the matron in charge and with reason.

My memory is not very clear on this episode in my childhood. I do not know why the father of the matron was in the home at all. Maybe, he was there to help out. The place was really in the middle of nowhere in rural Thueringen. The main building was large and spacious, but there were only two sleeping units. One unit was for the older children and the other was for the younger ones. I was with the older children. We were probably thirty in this unit. A teenager one evening told me that her father had sexually assaulted her. This was news to me and, luckily, it probably stayed with me in my subconscious.

I dragged behind my group at the afternoon outing because my knee started to hurt. The matron's father spotted me and offered to look at my knee. However, his hand went up my leg beyond my knee and tried to get underneath my panties. I panicked, pushed him away and run off after my group. The next day I was ordered to stay in bed all day and give my knee a rest. After lunch nobody was around, when I suddenly saw this old man walking towards my bed. Was I ever so scared! As he was lifting up my cover, the matron came from the other side and sternly asked him to leave. The next day after assembly I was commanded to come up front and before everybody I was pronounced a liar. I was really ashamed and so glad when Mama arrived to take us back home. Mama had good news: Dad was much better.

On Mama's next visit to the hospital, we came along and I was very upset to see so many soldiers with a missing leg or arm. However, none of them wanted to tell me about their heroic deeds for which they had received their medals. In looking through Dad's papers, I was most surprised to find that Dad, too, had received medals and a promotion from an ordinary soldier (Gefreiter) to an officer (Unteroffizier). At the time of my visit to the military hospital, I was very nasty to an amputee because he absolutely refused to tell me for which outstanding role he had received the Ritterkreuz (knight's cross). Of course I had to apologize and I still feel rotten about it.

Back home in the meantime, the bombing of the cities had intensified. I and the other five class mates were allowed to leave the camp when our troops were on the retreat from the advancing enemy armies. I went back with Mama and Regine to my aunts' farms. Mama stayed with Tante Christine, whose husband, Emil, was also in the army, but was on leave when we arrived. The slaughter of a pig was in progress. I saw him cut the pig's throat! A bucket was ready to receive the blood. I was horrified to learn that blood is the main ingredient of Blutwurst (blood sausage). During the slaughter, we were asked to be very quiet, because the farmers were only allowed to kill one pig a year for their own consumption and this was not the first. Apparently all the neighbours had done the same anyway. Yet, caution was now the order of the day.

As there was no room for all of us in Hundsbach, I went to my other aunt, Tante Marie. She had bought a small farm. However, there was a big modern house, a big yard, and a very large garden. The farm was at the end of the village in Buechold. The military base of Hammelburg was also nearby. The idea was that she would look after the farm and garden, and her husband, a carpenter by trade, would open a carpenter's shop in the yard. I went to the local school in Buechold where all the children were in one classroom. The younger children were in the front rows and the older ones in the back. Finally, I had a young pretty teacher. I liked her instantly, maybe because she had red hair just like my mother. Yet, she was not popular among the village folks. Was it because she was expecting a baby, but was not married? In my imagination, the pretty teacher had fallen in love with a dashing officer and she was waiting for him to come back after the war. Well, I hope he did. I was very happy at school and had lots of friends.

At that time, I had a crush on the boy next door. Funny that I suddenly remember his name! Hermann was a little older than me. He lived just across from us so I saw him often after school. He was taller than the other boys and had curly brown hair. He was very fond of his rabbits. He kept them in small cages at the side of the barn. One day I surprised him skinning a rabbit. I ran away as fast as I could: watching him skin the rabbit had killed my love for Herman.

Even we youngsters had to help with the war effort. After my eighth year at school, I had to do my duty for a year (Pfichtjahr). I had a choice: to work in a factory or on a farm.

As the mayor in the next small village, called Sachserhof, was looking for such a helper, he took me on the recommendation of the priest.

The thirteen big farms in this village were Erbgutsbauern, which means that these big farms could not be subdivided among siblings. This was in contrast to farms like my grandfather's, which were divided among siblings from one generation to the next and in the process got smaller in size. The oldest son or daughter in an Erbgutshof would inherit it all. The mayor of Sachserhof had two strong horses and some cows. He used the horses for his field work: the cows on his farm never left the barn, but were raised to give milk. On the other hand, the two cows my aunts had on their farms were used both to work in the fields and to give milk.

My contract did not include fieldwork, only housework. Nevertheless, I had to work side by side with the farmer, the Ukrainian maid, and the French prisoner of war. In the fields we weeded and used a hoe to loosen the soil between the rows of small plants. I could hardly keep up with the others. It was a hot spring and, in my ignorance, I did not drink enough, nor wear a hat, but I survived.

My boss in his role as mayor also had to accommodate the five French prisoners of war who worked in the hamlet on the farms. He would lock up their room at nine p.m. The jail had unlocked windows through which the Frenchmen would climb to freedom and visit the German women evacuated from the French/German border. Before dawn the prisoners of war would return to their jail. They were no trouble at all for the locals. I assume the Frenchmen were happy not be in the front line. I have no idea where the Ukrainian maid came from, but she was very nice, a good worker and I think she was only eighteen. She had to get up very early to arouse the cows for milking, which was done by hand and in a hurry, because the milk truck to pick up the cans of milk came early as well. Some of the animals did not want to get up and she had to be very cunning to make them stand up so she could work the udder. I hope she made it safely back to her homeland.

Daily I had to clean and cook a great pile of potatoes in a boiler for the many pigs the farmer kept. When feeding time came,

these creatures made an awful noise; they also smelled and fought for the food. When he was around, Arthur, the heir to the farm, usually fed them. Like a maid, I was made to wash the dishes and the kitchen floor and the hall daily. No wages and no thank-you did I receive; they had no manners whatsoever.

Sundays, was my day off. I cycled to Buechold to visit my aunt and her family. On the way there I stopped and went to Mass, followed by religious instructions. The large church stood on a small hilltop surrounded by a big cemetery. After Mass the women would attend to the graves, mainly planting flowers and watering them. They exchanged the latest news, while the men went to the nearby pub to drink. Other women would stay behind in church to pray the rosary for a certain person or cause.

The Wuerzburg area was also under aerial attack by the allied planes like other German cities. Their targets were the weapons factories located in this town. En route they flew directly over Buechold. At this spot the German anti-aircraft guns went into action and the dark sky was lit up as if by fireworks from the exploding shells. Dear Reader, it did have an effect on me, even though I was in no danger. I have never enjoyed watching fireworks. I never connected it to these events in my youth until last week when a reader in a letter to our newspaper wrote about his negative reaction to firework displays. He blamed these feelings on his war experiences. I cannot help but wonder about the reactions of veterans when they are reminded by events in their civilian life of their war experiences.

Soon afterwards, in 1945, World War II ended and my homeland was occupied by the American, British, French and Russians, who divided the defeated country into four military zones. The east zone was occupied by the Russians, who kept control of it for many years: the rest of Germany became the free country of West Germany. My family's home was in the south, in Frankfurt. My home town became the headquarters for the American army. The small modern high rise building was located in beautiful Rothschild Park. We were anxious to find out whether our apartment had survived the bombs. It was time for us to go back home. I volunteered to cycle to Frankfurt together with another teenager, via the Spessart mountains. We had cycled for some time passing here and there a lone German soldier on his way home when we ran into a check-point. We were asked by the American Military Police to return to our place of residence. They also reminded us that we were only allowed about six kilometers distance away from where we lived. I refused to turn back all this way which must have been about 150 km, but my friend did. By some luck, I discovered a forest road and was able to by-pass the Military Police check-point. Since I was cycling alone on a man's bike, I was in danger of having my vehicle taken away from me by one of the German escaped prisoners of war on his way home. I knew that all civilians had to be off the road at six o'clock and I was just in time to stop at my relatives in the next town of Offenbach.

I had visited my aunt Marie, my Dad oldest sister, before and was fairly familiar with the place. Of course I was welcome to stay with them as long as I wished. The big apartment was in an old city block and I could not see any destroyed houses at all. Elma and Renate, my two older cousins came home later. I had always admired them as both played the piano beautifully. Their dad, to my surprise, was there too - I do not know why he was not in the army. Was he suffering from some disability? Tante Marie encouraged him to show me his art work which was locked up in a display case. Unfortunately, I paid little attention to his art work because I was preoccupied with my down-to-earth problems. How do I get to Westhausen? In Offenbach, I was east of Frankfurt, but as the name implies, Westhausen is located on the west side and is right at the edge of town.

Luckily, there was already a bus line running. It went right through the middle of Frankfurt. The devastation down-town was complete; the few buildings still standing were beyond repair and were torn down later on. The historic Roemerplatz (Place of the Romans), where, according to local history, the Frankish king crowned himself as Karl der Grosse (Charles the Great) in about 800, was in ruin. My heart ached to see this destruction and my tears came when I saw German civilians shoveling the rubble aside in order to make a passage. These men and women out there looked like ghosts; the clothing they wore was too big for them and they looked pale and thin. To my relief, our apartment on the outskirts in Frankfurt was almost undamaged, although occupied by neighbors, who had moved in until their burned-out flat was restored. Moreover, they had not touched any of my mother's preserved food that was stored in the cellar. That was great news for us.

Soon afterwards, Onkel Emil returned home from and a few weeks later his son Franz. Both had lost a lot of weight. They slaughtered a pig and soon afterwards another. After having been on starvation rations, the digestion of both father and son could not cope with so much rich food. My uncle Emil died first, and soon afterwards his son followed him to the grave. Tante Christine had to look after the farm and her three young children who were all conceived when her husband came home on leave from the army.

My cousin, Ignaz, was sponsored by his relatives in the USA. They had a successful carpenter business in Union, New Jersey. I visited them soon after my arrival in Montreal in 1954. He had married a German girl by the name of Silke. They seemed to be happily married, except for one thing. She did not like it when all the male relatives were sitting together and drinking beer, while the whole Weber clan was spending the summer at their beach houses. After a while, Ignaz was drafted into the US Army.

About six months after his discharge, I heard of my cousin's death. Apparently it was an industrial accident. To this day I cannot believe it. What I presume is that my cousin took his own life. While his military unit did not go to Vietnam, he was trained to kill. Reader, I have no proof whatsoever, but now it is a fact that returning military from Afghanistan suffer from post-traumatic syndrome, (The Globe and Mail, June 25, 2012). Dear Reader I have also witnessed post-traumatic effects of the war in other members of my family, but I better leave it for later.

I have to add to the above the following news! I now have proof that Ignaz my cousin, committed suicide shortly after his return from military service in the United States Army. A member of the Weber family phoned me touch base again after nineteen years. Ulrike said that her Oma could not talk about her son's suicide. He had taken his own life. However, she also had good news, her Opa, Tante Marie's husband, did return from his service with the German Navy.

After we returned to our home near Frankfurt from the country, we commuted back and forth on *hamstern* trips (bartering clothing from the city in exchange for food from the country). Mama was very good at hamstern. She would visit her former friends from school for a chat and eventually ask them "are you interested in this silk blouse or maybe this silk dress"? Well, when there was interest, the matter of the price was discussed, which was in the form of food for us and the relatives in town. It was always a time-consuming journey but it seemed to be profitable. However, what was to be our last bartering trip was not profitable at all. No sooner had we arrived at the goods train terminal in Frankfurt, the air raid alarm sounded and the train passengers had to go in the bunker until the next morning. What a shock we had when it became light: thieves had gone off with Mama's dearly earned wares. Dear Reader, we did not go hamstern again.

A few weeks later, Dad stood outside the front door. He looked older and very thin. We were overjoyed to see him again. But it was not only Dad who had changed: Regine and I had grown up and were teenagers now. Mama realized immediately that he would need a lot of care. However it was not only his body that needed nourishment, but also his mind and soul. He was very quiet and did not answer our questions about his time in the army or about his release from the prisoner's camp.

Dad liked to be in our allotment garden by himself. However, as our garden was the first of about forty, other gardeners walking by would stop and make casual conversation and talk shop, e.g. how does your garden grow, etc.? Above all he liked to potter about. He had a big pile of dirt in the middle of our garden on which he threw all garden waste for composting. I guess he was one of the first organic growers of vegetables and the berries that grew on it. He was very proud of his produce. Nobody but him was allowed to pick his crop of sweet large berries. I suppose having been through the long depression before World War II, when food was not affordable for most people: he hated to see food wasted.

My plate had to be empty before I was allowed to leave the table. My mother sometimes took pity on me and took the plate away. Whereas most city folks looked down on farmers, he admired them. I now remember clearly what he said to me about my grandfather: "He cannot read nor write, but he is an excellent farmer". He gradually got over his melancholy and was ready to look for a job. He was not allowed to go back to his old job with the city of Frankfurt because his de-nazification process was not over yet.

In the fall Dad wanted to collect mushrooms in the near-by Taunus Mountains. A walk across the fields from Westhausen was long, but more interesting than the very long bus journey. The local mountains looked low in the distance but as we got closer the hills stood high in front before us. The Altkoenig was the second highest elevation of the Taunus. When we finally arrived there, the hills vanished. We were in a mixed forest dominated by oak trees. Some leaves had already fallen and we had to search for the precious mushrooms. Dad enjoyed these outings immensely. I enjoyed the comedy that followed at home as the crop was poured into a frying pan and Dad very carefully supervised the cooking process. He now had to decide between the poisonous and the eatable fungus. Mama did not always agree with him and there were heated arguments. The end result was that both Mama nor I had any at all. Nevertheless, I looked forward to the next walk over the fields to collect the precious crops.

More than anything, I liked to ski in the Taunus with Dad during his recovery from post-traumatic syndrome. He had done border control between Finland and Norway, the first few months of his military service. The skies I used, had been my bounty from Hammelburg, the military base. The skis were actually too long for me but there were no others.

I followed Dad in his tracks. He would always look out for me, stop, and watch me carefully coming towards him. He then demonstrated the correct style of doing the downhill. At one point, he suddenly bent down and showed me a stonewall emerging from under the snow. "Gudrun", he explained, "this is part of wall surrounding a fortress built by the Romans over a thousand years ago. We will go to the local museum on the site in the spring."

Our food rations were rather small, a job with meals provided would be ideal. So, like quite a few of his former colleges, Dad opted to work for the American forces, as a helper in the mess hall. Thus, he was able to bring home food for us as well, because there was always lots of waste. My mother, somehow obtained real American coffee with was used to get me and my sister new dresses. Dad had in effect healed himself from his depression through gardening. Voltaire, the French philosopher and author wrote on the last page of his book: "The Earthquake of Lisbon" that gardening is the best of all possible worlds. This insight has also been proven right.

Doing gardening as hobby was also a factor in the recovery from post-traumatic depression for my brother-in-law. Fred was only sixteen years old when he was drafted into the army towards the end of the war. By the end of his short training the Allied troops had invaded our country. Their tanks would push ahead and form a bridgehead waiting for the rest of the troops to catch up. Fred and his unit had to try to stop their advance by putting the tanks out of action. Their weapon was the Panzer Faust (tank grenade). Fred and comrades were taught

how to throw this special high explosive hand-grenade from close range at the passing tanks. I do not know how effective these newly invented weapons were, but he was taken prisoner by the Americans. He managed to escape and walked all the way home to Frankfurt. He must have been in constant fear of being picked up the Allies. I presume the fate of recaptured prisoners of war was death by shooting.

Fred met my sister, Regine, through a friend. Regine was being treated for tuberculosis and for more than a year was in a sanatorium, where Fred visited her. My sister's office was at the Hauptbahnhof (main railway station). At that time the locomotives were fueled by coal. All the buildings became black from the smoke of the locomotives. My sister's lungs became infected from the pollution. All of this was very disappointing for the two of us as we had planned that she would join me in Canada later.

Regine and Fred were married in 1957 soon after her release

from hospital and I went back to Frankfurt for their wedding. Fred worked as an environmental architect for the city of Frankfurt. He was a rather quiet man and liked to read. Like Dad, he had an allotment garden near their apartment. Fred was very happy there. He had put some garden furniture into their garden shed, where they made coffee and served cake. Regine always had a good show of flowers in the garden.

After Fred's retirement he took up painting. Regine was very supporting and it really became a hobby for both of them. Several paintings by him were shown at local exhibitions. Regine never mentioned to me or her two daughters that he was a problem for her. When Lilo, their younger daughter, was getting married, I flew to Frankfurt. I was surprised to hear that Fred had been admitted to a sanatorium for observation. Regine was reluctant to take me there, when I expressed my desire to visit him. I was shocked to see him completely changed. He did not acknowledge me and kept going around in circles like in a trance. I got very emotional seeing him in this

47

condition and had to leave quickly. To my surprise he had been given permission to attend the wedding ceremony but, fortunately, he did not show up. My sister died quite suddenly a few months later of lung cancer. Fred has been alone for over ten years now and is still enjoying his garden.

Dear Reader, I would like you to share an insight with me which I had during the night, when I really should have been asleep. I had come across the poems by suicidal Sylvia Platt, an American poetess. She had been married to an English poet, Ted Hughes: an ideal marriage many people assumed. Yet, Sylvia had a troubled soul. Reading her poetry is very upsetting for me. She had German parents. I believe that there must have been family secrets, which she dealt with through her poetry. I quote the poem "Daddy" (20th Century Poetry & Poetics. Second Edition. Verses 7 – end).

Daddy

An engine, an engine
Chuffing me off like a Jew.
A Jew to Dachau, Auschwitz, Belsen
I began to talk like a Jew.
I think I may well be a Jew.

The snows of the Tyrol, the clear beer of Vienna
Are not very pure or true.
With my gypsy ancestress and my weird luck
And my Taroc pack and my Taroc pack
I may be a bit of a Jew.
I have always been scared of you.
With your Luftwaffe, gobbledygoo.
And your neat moustache
And your Aryan eye, bright blue.
Panzer-man, O You _____

Not God but a swastika
So black no sky could squeak through.
Every woman adores a Fascist,
The boot in the face, the brute
Brute heart of a brute like you.

You stand on the blackboard, daddy,
In the picture I have of you,
A cleft in your chin instead of your foot
But no less a devil for that, no not
Any less the black man who

Bit my pretty red heart in two.
I was ten when they buried you.
At twenty I tried to die
And get back, back, back, to you.
I thought even the bones would do.

But they pulled me out of the sack.
And they stuck me together with glue.
And then I knew what to do.
I made a model of you,
A man in black with a Meinkampf look

And a love of the rack and the screw.
And I said I do, I do.
So daddy, I'm finally through.
The black telephone's off the root,
The voices just can't worm through.

If I've killed one man, I've killed two _____
The vampire who said he was you
And drank my blood for year,
Seven years, if you want to know.
Daddy, you can lie back now.

There's a stake in your fat black heart
And the villagers never liked you.
They are dancing and stamping on you.
They always knew it was you.
Daddy, daddy, you bastard, I'm through.

By the age of eighteen I could apply for my first office job with the American Forces to be trained as office personnel. It looked too good for me to pass up. I had no training at all for office work, so I grabbed the opportunity and applied. To my surprise, I was accepted. I ended my career in Germany as the private secretary to the head of the British Centre in Frankfurt.

During the six week training course in military correspondence, speed typing, English, and spelling, the trainees were assigned to a military unit. I worked up with the 7772 Signal Battalion, Special Services Section, in a nearby barrack, easily reached by streetcar from my home. The soldiers would sign out sports equipment and I had to hand it to them over the counter. I was very much puzzled by the baseball bat and the ball and wondered how a ball game could possibly be played with such an ill-matching pair. Well, I should really look up who invented baseball and why it is so popular in North America. "Not now, Gudy, you have a long way to go yet" says my inner voice!

I was glad when my six months with the military was up and I could start a job with British European Airways in their city office next to the Frankfurt Hauptbahnhof (main railway station). It was a very small office; therefore it was very crowded. The Englishman in charge of the city office obviously resented not having his own private office and we were glad when he left. Another newly-hired girl, Gerda, and I received tailor-made British European Airways uniforms and from now on, both of us were required to work at the airport. It was not always easy to get transportation with Dennis, our BEA English technical supervisor. The new car he had imported from back home was a lemon and a let-down for Dennis. The airport bus of American Airlines was only available for us when they had empty seats on board. By the way, American Airlines airline was running the Rhine-Main Airport's over-all operations and Dennis was courting Inge, the Station Superintendent's secretary. They got married after I left the airline. Thanks to BEA, Inge received from England the required medication for her diabetes. I heard later that she only lived a few more years. Apparently Dennis later married another German girl working at another airport.

A dispute between the Western Allies and Russia ensued. Russia intended to get what it wanted: closed the corridor in and out of West Berlin. The Allies decided to break the blockade and supplied Berlin with food and other necessaries from the air. To cut a long story short, Frankfurt became the American Forces supply base for West Berlin from June 1948 until Russia abandoned the blockade in May 1949.

During the blockade, civilian air traffic had to give priority to the military aircraft flying supplies to Berlin. Civilian airlines were hard-pressed to keep to their schedules and some of our British passengers were most annoyed when than they were late for their business meetings. The Berliners were most grateful to the Americans and, when John Kennedy visited Berlin after the war and said "Ich bin ein Berliner", the crowd, cheered him without end. It was too bad that he was murdered by a citizen of his own country.

I was very happy working at the airport. I was in charge of keeping the office files up-to-date, listening to all the announcements over the loudspeaker and being at the airfield when our two-engine Viking plane arrived from London to go on to Prague. Occasionally, nobody from AA was there to guide the plane in after it landed. It was my task, to do so. As the pilot and co-pilot got off the aircraft, I had to hand them the weather report which I had picked up before at the weather station. The airport at the time was tiny by comparison with what it is now. So it was an exciting time for me.

As you can see from my photo I had lots of freckles and I was

very conscious of them. I confessed to a fellow employee why I did not think that I was pretty. His answer made me very happy. "A face without freckles is like the sky without stars," he replied. I carried my head even higher from then on.

However, good things don't always last. Great Britain had a

monetary crisis and devalued its currency. Consequently, the staff was reduced. Herta and I had to hand in our tailor-made uniforms and left with crying hearts.

What next? I am very happy, dear Reader, to tell you that my luck continued. Strolling along the Kaiserstrasse near the Hauptbahnhof, I spotted an unfamiliar sign: "British Centre". Curiously, I went upstairs and a receptionist approached me. "Yes" she said, "we are newly opened and are looking for more staff. We are like the Amerika Hause you have here in Frankfurt. In the British Zone of Germany this institution is called British Centre. The British Centre here in Frankfurt will be the only one in the American zone." Early on Monday morning I showed up at the Centre. Mrs. Tonges smiled and called the boss. He carefully read my references from the American Military Forces and British European Airways, nodded his head and said I could start tomorrow as a receptionist and reading room attendant. Mrs. Tonges would show me everything.

In the reading room we had the major English newspapers on the day of their publication by one o'clock. Of the many magazines my favorite was the Illustrated London News. The news from the British Common-wealth at the time stirred my imagination and opened new horizons for me (photo). Teachers and students from the nearby Berlitz School of Languages frequently came in to read. One of the teachers told me that the school was going on a bus trip to Paris and asked if I would be interested to go along.

I had never been outside Germany and to go to Paris was beyond my dreams. I invited my friend Margot who became equally excited as I was. For one reason or the other, the driver went not on the highway but took bumpy country roads instead. Looking out of the bus window, I was amazed at the old neglected small homes of the French farmers. Through the open door I could see lots of chicken running around in their living room. I, too, had lived in the country but never had I seen such primitive living conditions in any of our villages.

I cannot remember having seen any signs of the war as we entered Paris. I was getting disappointed with France, but seeing Paris left me and Margot awestruck. An exact account of what happened was reported in the Vancouver Sun newspaper recently. On August 25, 1944, Paris was liberated after four years of Nazi occupation. Adolf Hitler had ordered the city razed, but General Dietrich von Choltitz chose to ignore his command and surrendered his force of 17,000 men to the Allies. The liberation wasn't all peaceful; fierce fighting went on for several days in the streets of Paris between the German soldiers and the French resistance. The Germans had occupied Paris for four years and left it undamaged.

The Cathedral of Notre Dame was on our list. The twin towers looked inviting. Many steep steps were spiraling up a narrow tower. Breathless, Margot and I arrived at the top and sat down exhausted on the roof.   The view over Paris was excellent. Suddenly, there was a terrific noise near us. The Bells of Notre Dame were ringing the hour of the day: 12 o'clock.   There were no angels up here to protect us from falling off the steep roof, only frightening gargoyles. On leaving the cathedral, we admired the huge rose window in stained glass in one of the portals. My memory fails me as to how long we stayed in Paris and what else we saw.

I have been to Paris several times since then. I hope to return again to visit the cemetery where famous poets and other artists are buried. It is located right in the middle of Paris. I was very touched to see that the grave of Heinrich Heine (1799-1856), the German-Jewish lyric poet, was decked out with real flowers left by his many admirers. No live flowers could be seen in the entire cemetery. He married a simple French girl who looked after him as he was immobilized by paralysis. His poems were easy to read but had so much meaning. Among them is the "Song of the Lorelei" (the Lorelei is a beautiful mermaid who sits on a high cliff. The sailors go sailing by look up to her, and do not see the treacherous waters of the Rhein, consequently the sailors drown).

In Exile.

Once upon a time I had a fine country of my own
where I was at home.
The oaks grew tall there,
the violets beckoned gently.
It was a dream.

It kissed me in German and said in German
– It is hard to believe how good it sounded –
the words "I love you".
It was only a dream.

(Penguin Book of German Verse. Translated and edited by Leonard Forester).

Well, dear Reader, Heinrich Heine did not live in my time. Yes, I was homesick myself, especially in the first few years, but not since I arrived here in Vancouver.

We also had unwanted visitors in the Reading Room of the British Centre. One of the duties I did not enjoy doing was to ask these visitors to leave the premises. These were still hard times in the early Fifties and accommodation was difficult to come by, so these men came in from the street to warm themselves.

The director, who had hired me, was replaced by another. Mr. Renter was in his early seventies and a retired professor, but he acted very young. We always knew when he was coming, because he was the only one who ran up the flight of stairs. We all liked him. After a few weeks Mr. Renter asked me if I took shorthand. I replied that I did, but that it had become rusty. He encouraged me to brush it up. A short time afterwards he called me into his office and gave me a test. "Well," he said, "You will do". What a stroke of good luck I had there. The boss was a non-smoker but his secretary was a chain smoker, so she got my job and I was given hers. As simple as that, but it had a sad ending, nevertheless. His former secretary died a year later of cancer. When she was in hospital, we took turns in visiting her. I was shocked to see her so thin and bald, and I kept in the back of the room. However, I felt a great pity for her and vowed not to smoke.

I was not very busy working for my new boss, but I needed my wits to transcribe correctly from my steno pad. Mr. Renter had been invited by the Goethe University to give a lecture on T. S. Elliot's poem "The Waste Land." His dictation was slow and clear, but I did not understand what it was all about. The poem was dictated to me over a couple of days piecemeal, and the fact that he always left his notes and books on his desk, helped me to transcribe it more or less. As time went by I got good at it and gained more confidence. Here is the poem. (T. S. Elliot in The Norton Anthology of Poetry Revised. Page 1034.)

The Waste Land

The Burial of the Dead.

April is the cruellest month, breeding
Lilacs out of the dead land, mixing
Memory and desire, mixing
Dull roots with spring rain
Winter kept us warm, covering
Earth in forgetful snow, feeding

Summer surprised us, coming over the Starnbergersee
With a shower of rain; we stopped in the colonade,
And went on in sunlight, into the Hofgarten
And drank coffee, and talked for an hour.
Bin gar keine Russin, stamm' aus Litauen, echt deutsch'.
And when we were children, staying at the archduke's,
My cousin's, he took me out on a sled,
Marie, hold on tight. And down we went.
In the mountains there you feel free.
I read, much of the night, and go south in the winter.

Mr. Renter frequently had visitors from England and I was always asked to make tea. The kitchen was through the cinema. Our films were very popular with our visitors and not because they were free, but because they were topical and interesting. For instance, at the coronation of Queen Elizabeth, people lined up around the block to get in and we had to extend the showing for an extra week. But I was going to make tea! Well, it always took me quite a while before I returned to the office with my tray. After I poured the tea the English way, that is, the milk first, I was asked to leave. I never found out at the time why these men just dropped in. In hindsight I now can guess. Dear Reader, have you ever read Le Carre's novels? "The Spy who came in from the Cold" made the author famous. The book was even made into a movie; it remains one of my favorite classical movies. If this was the case, dear Reader, I was kissed by a spy!

My over-seventy-years-old boss took me, as a farewell treat, for lunch to a fancy restaurant in the Frankfurter Stadtwald. At the end he gave me a peck on my cheek and wished me good luck for my journey to the new world. Oh, oh, and who could I see sitting in the corner of the dining room? Yes, my dear friend, you guessed it: another spy? I had often wondered how this daily reader to our Centre found the time to sit around for hours reading the daily English newspapers and magazines.

Well, this seemed like a true-to-life version of: "Tinker, Taylor, Sailor, Spy", one of Le Carre''s novels. Of course, it might have been all my vivid imagination, but my instinct tells me that it is true.

We also had a Press office in our Centre headed by a Press Officer. Mr. Nickols was a dashing-looking tall man. However, his Italian wife outdid him. They had met in the war and he was writing a book about it. He quite often dropped in and asked me to type his drafts. Unfortunately, he never finished his love story: he suffered a heart attack while playing tennis. Rumour had it that the heart attack was not brought on by the strain of playing tennis, but by shock. He had seen his wife at the other end of the courts playing tennis with his best friend.

Adolf, the German secretary in the Press office, was a real character. He was a nudist and went off on his Vespa almost every weekend to the camp. When he returned to the office on Mondays he showed off his physique: chest out, stomach pulled in; he danced about the office, but he was really a good fellow. He did not mind when I refused his invitation to come with him to the nudist camp because I was a Catholic. We also had a sad case in Centre. We all liked Mrs. Krone for one reason or the other. She had met her husband in the war. He was a pilot in the German air force. Three months after they had married, he was reported missing. Mrs. Krone and her baby moved in with the in-laws and they were all still waiting for the missing pilot to return. She had many admirers but could not re-marry because her husband was never reported dead. I learned later that she took to the bottle.

Mrs. Renter was an experienced hostess. She knew how to keep her guests entertained. We learned to play Charades and I became good at it. At Christmas, their son, Bill, came to Frankfurt from boarding school in England with a friend. We all got along very well. As you can see, dear Reader, from the enclosed photos we were a happy lot. Later on I was glad to have had the English experience of playing games, and how to pour tea, when I married an Englishman and lived in England for a short time.

Dear Reader, you may wonder by now why I wanted to travel to the new world? I loved my job, but I also wanted to have "a place of my own". However, in postwar Germany "a place of one's own" was not available yet. The City Planning Department had big visions; from the ruins of the old town a modern city would rise; the narrow streets must make room to accommodate cars and underground garages. Equally, citizens required homes to live in; historic buildings, like the Cathedral and the gates of the former walled old town had to be restored and the owners of the properties had to be paid for the appropriation of their property. I could not wait. The immigration office pointed out to me that I had a good job and asked me why I wanted to emigrate. My answer was that I never, ever, wanted my sons to have to live or even fight in a war like the last one. That satisfied him. He stamped my passport, stood up, shook my hand and wished me good luck.

In retrospect however, I think that my motives to go to the New World, were also fuelled by the subconscious desire to meet the native Indians. In my early teens I had been very ill and our next door neighbor brought over stacks of books by German author Karl May, because her daughters had moved out. I read day and night forgetting my aches and pains and was very content to lie in bed accompanying the noble, but fictional Winnetou on his adventures. My childhood fascination with the Wild West stories was not an isolated case. It spread throughout Germany and reached new heights after I had arrived in the Wild West proper.

When I returned home from our recent Panama cruise, our oldest son Peter, with a mischievous look, handed me an article from a monthly American literature magazine and said with an ironic smile: "There is an excellent article for you to read, Mum"! And he was right. I learned that yearly Karl May festivals are held near the town of Bad Segebad in Germany. It goes on and describes in detail the Disneyland-like Wild West show. This goes far beyond of what I had experienced during my university years in the late seventies. How the Germans see the rest of the World was to be the theme of one of my literature courses. On the reading list to my surprise I read "Winnetau". I finally meet my hero again in the most unexpected place. My dear Reader, no longer am I ashamed of having been in love with Winnetau after all, he seems to have been loved by millions of other romantic people in my former homeland.

According to the writer of the article Wild West Germany in The New Yorker dated April 9, 2012 the first Karl May festival was near Bad Segebad. The cost to put it on was only twelve thousand dollars, whereas today it has climbed to 3.9 million euros. I had no idea that films had also been made about the Wild West stories of Karl May, with well-known actors. My English-born husband has just mentioned that in his school the "houses" were all named after Indian tribes, but the name, Karl May, was not then known to him. By the way, I got an "A" in this subject.

How to tell my mother that I was going away? As expected, it was not easy. To my surprise, however, she was well informed. "Oh", she said, "in Kanada, dort ist keiner da". [In Canada there is nobody]. Indeed, looking at the statistics of the vastness of this country and its small population, my mother was as usual, quite right.

PART II.

My Journey to the New World started on the 14th of May in 1954. The boat left Bremerhafen full of immigrants to Canada. I was disappointed to find that some of the passengers had not paid for their voyage, but were sponsored by Charitas, a religious organization, while I had paid the fare from my savings. I enjoyed the crossing immensely. I even developed a liking to a very nice young man. To my disappointment he turned out to be a Catholic priest. I arrived in the New World on my own.

I had, however, a contact in Montreal. Mrs. Tonges, who was a war widow, had also journeyed to the New World with her twelve year old daughter. She was at the train station in Montreal and advised me where to find accommodation. She lived in the university district close to Mount Royal. I was able to get a sitting-room with bath almost across the street from her. My landlord kindly offered to get my very big trunk from the railway station. My next step was to contact the Government Employment Office. Were they expecting me? I was asked to report to the Telegraph Office of the National Railways. It was a very large office under the railway tracks which led from the station to the docks. The boss sat behind a desk from which he could see everyone. I was not going to be his secretary: he already had one named Anna. Since GUDRUN was difficult to pronounce, Anna had the bright idea to shorten my name to GUDY. This is the name I still go by. Anna was full of information.

This Canadian Telegraph Office was unionized and had certain rules under which the employees had to abide by or be dismissed on the spot. For instance, you must not get married. I could not believe my ears. Where was I? In a democratic society these rules were hard to understand. However, it got worse outside. At a nearby Pub a sign over the entrance warned "Men and Escorts" and on another "Men only", maybe a toilet, I wondered. However, I was most surprised to find a sign which read "Gentiles only". Where was I? I questioned myself again. I thought I had escaped racism by coming to Canada, but apparently not. The lunch-hour break was long enough for me to walk sometimes to a small family-run restaurant, which served very good French pea soup for seventy five cents, bun included. At other times, I brought my own sandwiches.

When winter came, I bought myself a fur coat on the advice of Mrs. Tonges. The coat turned out to be a necessity and not a luxury. It got really cold. The snow gave me new outlets. I shared an apartment with Monique, friend of mine, who showed me the steps to climb, which ended on top of Mount Royal, where there was a panoramic view of Montreal. We were lucky to spot the two police sleighs. The police allowed us to take a photo with them.

Dear Reader, I have to tell you of an incident which really hurt my

German national pride. Monique and I shared a two-bedroom apartment. I had met her at night classes and she suggested that we should share. I was happy to do so because she was French Canadian and I hoped to improve my French. To my great disappointment I could not understand one word when her sister came to visit; they came from Sherbrooke and the French spoken there is different from the French spoken in Montreal, not to mention Paris! Anyway, the tiny kitchen in our shared apartment was in my bedroom behind a wall. When I was sitting one winter's evening doing my homework, I suddenly saw horrible looking insects crawling in a long line from under the kitchen door towards me. I frantically called out for Monique to come; she looked at them, turned around and said calmly: "German cockroaches". Well, I never, ever, saw these bugs back in Germany. Apparently they are commonly found in damp hot places and, because of the very cold weather in Montreal, windows stay locked in winter and it gets warm, but the rooms also get damp from the cooking.

After six months with the CNR, I was eligible for a free railway pass. My boss was not in favor of my plan to travel to Vancouver. He said that he had been for six weeks in Vancouver on a course and it had rained every day. However, nothing could stop me. I had had enough of Montreal where there was so much tension between the French-speaking and English-speaking population, as well as the new ethnic immigrants. At the last minute I postponed my trip out West as our office was moving from Montreal to Toronto into a brand new building right next to the Railway Station. Yes, the offer to the staff to transfer included me as well. How generous, I thought.

It would have been hard for me to say good bye to my dear friends, Herta and Rolf at that time. I cannot remember where we actually met in Montreal, but this does not matter. Rolf spoke only French which was to his disadvantage because he wanted a job in the auto industry. Herta spoke very little French or English. She found work in a factory making zippers; the pay was seventy five cents an hour. They actually succeeded in moving to the United States. I visited them in Cleveland, Ohio, years later on my honeymoon; they lived in their own house in a nice neighborhood. When living in Montreal they drove to a little hotel at a lake in the Laurentian Mountain on weekends. They very kindly invited me to come along and to this day I am very grateful to them.

The Laurentian Mountains were a favorite get-away for the residents of Montreal in summer and winter. I seem to have been there in the winter as well, but I only remember it having been very cold, I must have skied. Yes, I did. In the summer the city of Montreal was sticky and unbearably hot. In fact, my other friend who shared the upstairs rooming house and I slept outside on the fire escape which every house in downtown Montreal was required to have. The Laurentians were the right place to be in the summer. On the way there, I enjoyed the ride through the rural French communities. It surprised me to see that, in spite of the terrific cold winters, the Canadian houses were all built of wood. Like so many houses elsewhere, they had huge verandas on the ground floor. However, only here in rural Quebec the older folks would sit in rocking chairs, while the younger generation would run about playing happily with each other in spite of the heat and the swarms of mosquitoes.

The office staff who accepted the transfer offer from the Canadian National Telegraph were given one week free stay at the Royal York Hotel to give them time to find accommodation. Boy, I felt like a big shot! I found a place on a nice tree-lined street near a subway station. In only ten minutes I was at my new office. The rooming house turned out to be a great place to be. There were about twelve girls living in bed-sitting rooms; a big kitchen was downstairs in the basement. It was in the shared kitchen where the fun began.

Even though I find the American expression "girls" very odd when it is used for older females, it was appropriate here. Among us were three Australian girls who were on the Grand Tour of Canada and Great Britain. The tour was popular with other Aussies as well. They arrived on the big P&O passenger ships that used to come from Australia to Vancouver, and found themselves jobs to earn travel money to take them to their next stop-over. After Toronto they crossed the Atlantic to explore the land of their fathers and mothers before returning back home to Australia, unless they had met a mate-for-life en route.

The Belgian girl was anxiously waiting for permission to go to the Congo and the rest of them were not that interesting to me, because I cannot remember their stories, except for the only Canadian among us foreigners. Let us call her Betty. We were more or less vegetarians except for her. The bigger and bloodier the steak was the more she liked to it. "You are what you eat" was her argument. Well, she certainly was a big strong looking girl;

every Friday evening she was picked up and on Sunday night returned, looking happy, but, unfortunately, the joy did not last all week. The only phone in the rooming house was outside her bed-sitting room. We all knew that she was listening to our telephone conversations from the inside of her room. Usually these conversations were boring. But not when my roommate Francis was speaking with her husband. Like Monique in Montreal, I had met her at night class. She was also a French Canadian, but came from Quebec City. She was married to a Hungarian student who was in his last year at university. They were living at his parent's house. The inevitable happened; she did not get on with her in-laws. In the end Francis moved in with me. Unfortunately, her husband did not pass his examination and she got the blame. That was the last straw; she moved down to Florida because at the time one could not get a divorce in the Province of Quebec. I had really liked both of them.

I badly needed a rest as the break-up of their marriage had drained me emotionally. I joined the three Australian girls on their trip to

Washington D.C. As I had not been involved in the travel arrangements, I have no idea how the girls were able to get us into the White House on the day after our arrival. I felt so honored to be admitted to the place where President Dwight Eisenhower was working. We were not rushed through the Oval Office. My imagination got the better of me and I saw the famous former General sitting behind the big desk over there, looking through the pile of papers. Finally he answered the phone, and stood up to receive a foreign-looking delegation, which was coming through the door. Leaving the White House, we stopped on the white marble stairs to take a picture.

The girls had only come for the weekend but I had taken a few days off. Making the most of my extra time in Washington, I sat out early next morning to explore this beautiful city by walking down a wide avenue which had a huge monument in the distance. On reaching the monument, I read that it was in honor of President Abraham Lincoln (1805-65). Like President John Kennedy, he was murdered in his own country.

Beside me was a young uniformed man. It turned out that he was a West Point cadet and together we read the inscriptions. Along the way he informed me about the highlights of the Lincoln presidency. I was very impressed by the politeness of this young American. He didn't chew gum unlike the GIs I had met in Germany. I followed his recommendation and went by bus to the Arlington Cemetery across on the other side of the Potomac River. The changing of the Guard brought tears to my eyes, remembering all of these young men who died serving their country. I was also very emotional when I visited much later a cemetery in Belgium with my young family. I have recently come across a poem by John McCrae and I feel it is a good place to quote it here:

In Flanders Fields

In Flanders Fields the poppies blow
Between the crosses, row on row,
That mark our place; and in the sky
The larks, still bravely singing, fly
Scarce heard amid the guns below.
We are the Dead, Short days ago
We lived, felt dawn, saw sunset glow,
Loved, and were loved, and now we lie
In Flanders fields.

Take up our quarrel with the foe:
To you from failing hands we throw
The torch; be yours to hold it high.
If ye break faith with us who die
We shall not sleep, though poppies grow

Canada Veterans Affairs Canada. "Canada in the First World War and the Road to Vimy Ridge."

I felt rather depressed on the way to my hotel in Washington. I decided therefore to stay only one more day. I remember going to the Smithsonian Museum, because it was close-by and looked at lots of stamps, but I was not happy to be by myself. Somehow I did not feel safe anymore. Early the next day I boarded the train and arrived back in Toronto, where the girls and I had lots to talk about regarding our visit to the White House.

It was time for me to move on and I got my free return railway pass. Canada's distances, five thousand miles from the Atlantic coast to the Pacific Coast are overwhelming for a European traveler. The emptiness of the Prairies has to be experienced and the Rocky Mountains have simply to be enjoyed. As the train rolled along, my favorite lookout place was the last carriage. I would sit there early in the morning to see day break and until late into the evening to watch darkness arrive.

Dear Reader, as I type this draft of my journal into my new laptop computer, I am passing through the Panama Canal on a cruise with Holland America Line. A writer called the Canal: "A Path through the Sea". The canal was also called: "The Eighth Wonder of the World". The Canal truly deserves all these attributes, but how about the building of the Canadian National and Canadian Pacific Railways through the Rocky Mountains, which truly is "Path through the Mountains"? It is also an engineering triumph just like the building of the Panama Canal, but does not carry such clout. On my way West at the time, I was still an inexperienced traveler and not informed about the history of the Canadian railways: I just enjoyed the ride as most passengers do. However I will go into it shortly.

Another friendly Canadian on board invited me for dinner in the dining room carriage, Alaska smoked cod was my choice. I had never tasted such a delicacy. The nice nurse from Victoria was expected: a handsome man kissed her as she got off the train. He probably was a doctor from a Victoria hospital coming all the way to Vancouver to welcome her. Suddenly, I became a little bit jealous and felt very lonely.

Here is short history of the building of the railway through the Canadian Rocky Mountains. At the same time, I will give you a short history of the building of the Panama Canal. ("The National Dream" The Great Railway 1871-1881. Pierre Berton: "The Path between the Seas." The Creation of the Panama Canal 1870-1940). Both books give you the full details of the their history.

For both ventures, the natural environment itself posed great obstacles for such an undertaking at the time: the walls of the Canal kept sliding into the bottom of the trench and blocked the passage; whereas the hard rock of the steep mountain slopes and canyons of the Rockies seemed to be completely impassable. Solutions for the undertakings had to be found, as too much was at stake. A shortcut through the continent would eliminate sailing all the way around stormy Cape Horn. The building of the Railway through the Rocky Mountains was to join the Colony of British Columbia to the Dominion of Canada.

A shortage of a skilled workforce plagued both projects from the start. In the beginning some of the unemployed from Europe came when the French were digging the canal. Among them was Paul Gauguin, who later bought some land on an island in the Pacific and painted the native women in a post modernism style which made him famous. Eventually, the United States government took over the construction and the military were ordered by the President to finish the canal project. Where others had failed, the military forces succeeded and the Panama Canal opened in 1914, just before the outbreak of World War I. There was much to be gained by building the Canal and the Railway. A shortcut joining the seas would eliminate sailing all the way the way around stormy Cape Horn at the southern tip of South America and save the ships a distance of 9,000 Miles. The building of the railway through the Rocky Mountains was to join the Colony of British Columbia to the Dominion of Canada.

Labourers were brought from as far away as China by the private

Canadian Railway Company to work on their project. Two ships full of the Chinese had a bad crossing and all the passengers had to stay under deck. The heavy work the men had to do so soon after their arrival resulted in the men developing scurvy and many of them died of the decease. Yellow fever was responsible for many deaths in Panama. Its source was then unknown. Catholic nuns operated a hospital in a swampy area. Medical scientists eventually discovered the source of the disease: the mosquitoes which bred in the swamps. Of the twenty four nuns who cared for the sick and dying in the hospital, only four survived. Diseases caused many other workers to die. Medical researchers eventually discovered how to fight yellow fever as well as other tropical diseases. It is said that between twenty-five and thirty thousand people died in building the Canal.

Dynamite was essential to blast both a path between the seas and a railroad through the Rocky Mountains. In both cases it was achieved with a loss of many lives through accidents. I traveled through the Rocky Mountains in 1955 and through the Panama Canal in 2011 and again in 2012. Now a widening of the canal is progressing rapidly and should be finished on time: 2014. The railway track through the mountains needs to be looked after by work crews throughout the year. Rockslides, snowdrifts, derailments and other accidents still happen year round.

Dear Reader, in hindsight I realize that the CNR Superintendent of Works, where I had replaced an employee for a short time, was in fact in control of these work crews. I sometimes saw wild-looking men drop in to converse with him. On several occasions he himself would be away for a few days. In fact, dear Reader, I am tickled pink to remember the connection fifty-eight years later.

Many passengers on this cruise ship are looking forward to visiting Stanley Park. The Park is still the number one attraction in Vancouver. Drivers have to pay if they stop in the Park and people have to pay if they play tennis. Everything was free when I arrived in Vancouver. Stanley Park became the playground of the immigrants; most of them found accommodation close to the park, as I did. The house I moved into was quite a stately- looking home owned by an English bachelor. He had an elderly English housekeeper, who came in during the day only. The upstairs two apartments he rented out. He seemed to like me and I liked him. We had an English sherry together and I moved in the next day. From a little window in the large kitchen I could even see the sunset over English Bay.

Eventually, I met my elderly neighbour and she took me to the races. It was all very new to me. The horses she backed did not win at the races, but she was not discouraged and she invited me to come with her again. One morning I heard knocking in the house, as I rushed off to work but did not think much of it. When I came home in the evening, I still heard it, more faintly and less frequently. I called the housekeeper. She opened my neighbour's door, looked in and called the ambulance. My neighbour did not survive. Would she have been saved, if help would have come to her earlier?

The West End of Vancouver at my time had very few high-rise apartments. Accommodation for new-arrivals was in private homes, either upstairs under the roof or downstairs in the basement. There were not many cars in the street on the way to work; everybody went by bus, it seemed. It took me only about twenty minutes to get to the office at the railway station. Here, too, the boss was sitting upfront facing us. We were only about ten employees in this office. Nobody bothered to explain to me what the Superintendent's office was all about because I was only temporary. It was not a happy place. The area around the railway station was also run down, except for a small park with a lawn and flower beds around it. I cashed my pay check at the bank down the street. The only pedestrians I saw were old bent Chinese men: the imported workforce for building the railway. Their families were not allowed to join them here in Canada. I was told that they met in basements at night to gamble. Somehow, I was not comfortable meeting them on the same sidewalk, so for safety I crossed over to the other side of the street.

Let us take a break here, dear Reader, and talk about something entirely different to cheer me up. After Sunday Mass at our small Catholic church in West Vancouver our new priest sometimes joins members of the congregation downstairs for refreshments. He is still trying to learn our names. On the Sunday before we left to go on our cruise to Alaska, he suddenly turned to me saying that he had met another Gudrun and could I please tell him where the name came from. Dear Reader, I have done some more research and decided to tell you about it as well, because it is so interesting.

"Das Nibelungenlied" is a heroic poem, author unknown, written about 1200 A.D. The epic as it concerns my name, Gudrun, originated in Iceland. When the poem reached the Germanic-

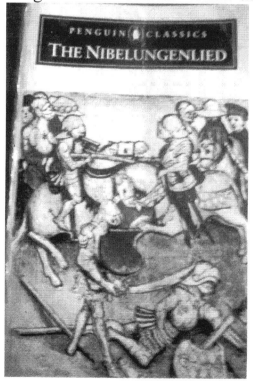

speaking people to the south, Gudrun appeared as Krimhild in the tale. In the plot is Siegfried, who wanted to marry beautiful Krimhild. However, her oldest brother, Hagen, was against it for reasons of his own. Siegfried was favored by the Gods and had been made immortal. His body had been anointed with dragon blood. Unfortunately, one tiny spot at one heel had been missed. Hagen knew this. One day, Hagen aimed his arrow at the unprotected spot and killed Siegfried. When Krimhild heard this, she swore revenge.

The revenge committed by her alone, was really very cleverly done. She invited her kindred to come to the court of Attila, whose hand in marriage she had accepted, to celebrate their union. After her three brothers had also arrived with all their knights and were sitting in the great hall, drinking and cheering each other, Krimhild locked all the doors and set fire to the wooden building. No one escaped. Afterwards she fell into a deep depression and wanted to commit suicide, so she went into the river and tied rocks to her feet. However, the current carried her downstream to a shore, where she was rescued. The ruler of this kingdom married the beautiful Krimhild and she bore him three sons. Unfortunately, none of the sons died a natural death. (Penguin Classics "The Niebelungenlied" front cover detail from the Hundeshagen Codex, reproduced by permission of the Striftung Preussischer Kulturbesitz, translated by A. T. Hatto.)

Revenge by killing the murderer was accepted at the time of the Niebelungenlied. However, under the influence of the Romans, who extended their empire to the north i.e. into Germany and as far as England, outright revenge was now replaced by the written law of the Romans. Charles the Great, who crowned himself at the Roemer in Frankfurt in 800, also had the blessings of the Pope in Rome. Naturally, the subjects under him became Christians. Now monasteries and their schools blossomed. The monasteries received gifts of land and become rich. With the building of Cathedrals and human settlements, the Middle Ages had arrived. Why my parents chose Gudrun as my name, I do not know.

The German Composer Richard Wagner (1813-1883) set to music the heroic epic, called it "Die Walkuer" and gave it his own interpretation. The opera is in three parts; each part takes a whole evening and may play for a week or longer. The Seattle Opera Company, Washington, USA, plays one part of the opera for their whole season. I have seen a modern production of the "Die Walkuer" at Convent Garden in London, England, and thought it was awful. To my surprise, the press the next day was on my side.

However, the same opera section in a traditional production in Frankfurt, which I attended during a visit, was supreme and received a standing ovation from the audience. Richard Wagner is accused by some critics for his anti-Semitism (MacLean's Magazine August 12, 2009) but he was not anti-feminist. This part of the opera "Der Ring", deals with female warriors who come down from Walhal to take the corpses of the fallen heroes back to Walhal. I personally would not travel to see "The Ring" cycle, but I would consider a visit to a performance, if it was on the theatre program of a town I was in. "The Flying Dutchman", a legend of redemption through a female, is another often performed opera by Wagner, and appeals to me much more, as the music is mostly about the raging sea and not long drawn arias liked The Ring.

I must continue with my journal and deal with my situation in Vancouver. After the clerk came back from her leave of absence, I had no job. Office Overload took care of me as a temporary help; the pay was $1.25 an hour. I must have been a long time in one office but my memory is hazy as to where. I would not have recalled Norah if it had not been for her photo in my album. At Christmas she invited me to her home. Sweeny, her husband had his own small business, he was a very good drummer on the side. She had eloped with him. Was it for this reason that her parents were not there? Another man was sitting at the piano playing a tune. After the introduction he wanted me to sing: "Lilly Marlene", a well-known song of both World Wars:

> *Vor der Kaserne, vor dem grossen Tor,*
> *steht eine Laterne*
> *und steht sie noch davor…*

As now, I had difficulties to remember the rest of the song. It might be, dear Reader, that you know it? I read in a popular historical novel "The Fall of Giants" that Lilli Marlene was sung at Christmas by both sides in the trench-war. The officers from both sides met and shook hands with each other. Some were also related to each other, through the British Queen Victoria. The clever queen had married off her many daughters to the ruling kings and princes in Europe. Although these heads were cousins, it did not prevent the soldiers of these countries from fighting each other in World War I. The kings were just figureheads.

Sweeny and Norah also invited me to go skiing with them to Mount Baker in Washington State just south of the Canadian border. We left early, but were slowed down at the border, where I had to go to passport-control to fill out forms. I was not a Canadian yet. I did not go up the steep two-seat gondola, but stayed at the bottom to do cross-country skiing in the deep snow. I was totally exhausted by the time we left the mountain. Again, I had to delay them by spending some time at passport-control. However, my image improved somewhat, when I shared my home-made sandwiches with them. Sweeny had a Cuban connection. When his friend moved there, he rented out his luxury house to them. Like in the Gebrueder Grimms Fairy Tales, Sweeny and his beautiful wife, Norah, appear to have lived "happily ever after".

One day the principal from Office Overload said to me that one of her clients was considering employing a permanent secretary. I went for the interview and got the job at a middle-sized law firm in downtown Vancouver. The lawyer I worked for did contracts for a builder who operated out of Calgary. Our beautiful Bay Shore Inn at the entrance to Stanley Park was on the drawing board. I did not have to know anything about law. It was a nice office with a view of the harbour. The attached library was impressive. I could eat my home-made sandwiches there. The top lawyer in this firm often went to Court and his secretary was always very busy. I admired her in many ways.

When our junior lawyer needed a secretary, Janet was hired. She had recently arrived from England with her boyfriend, a newly qualified English lawyer. He could not find employment in the depressed Vancouver area, so he went up North. He had asked his friend David to look after Janet while he was away. Janet and I decided to move in together, as we could then afford a place with a view of Sunset Beach. When I moved in, climbing up the steep stairs in the ill-lit hallway, an English voice said to me: "Let me help you with your heavy box. My name is David and I am here to help Janet. You must be Gudy, her new roommate". I liked his voice and soon I liked him, as well. After a visit to a play, we went out to dinner. David asked me the date of my birthday: "December 16", I replied. A long pause followed. "Can you prove it?" I showed him my passport and he said: "So is mine". It was the beginning of another fairytale by the Brothers Grimm. If you care to know the ending of this fairytale, dear Reader, look out for my second book in a year's time around Christmas 2013. In the meantime, take care.

20206183R00045

Made in the USA
Charleston, SC
01 July 2013